GENRE readers' & writers' WORKSHOP™

BIOGRAPHY

George Washington

Abraham Lincoln

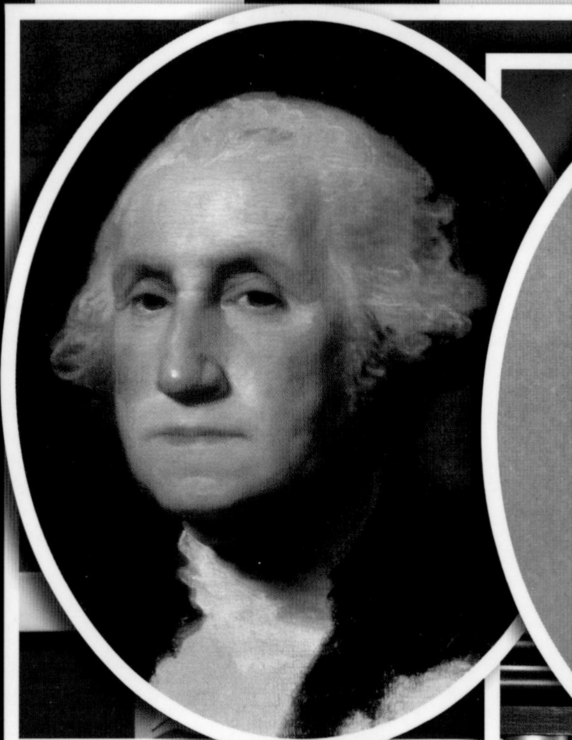

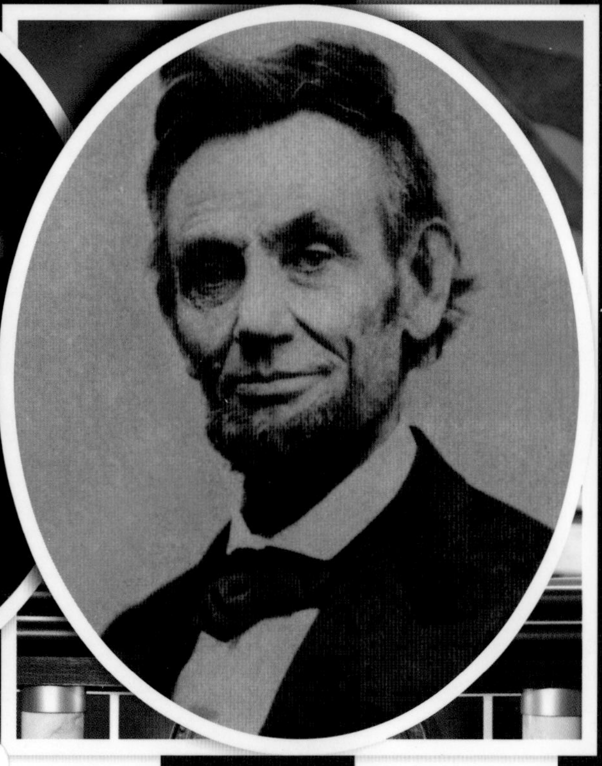

by Catherine Goodridge

GENRE: Biography

LITERARY ANALYSIS

- Respond to and interpret text
- Make text-to-text connections
- Analyze the genre

READING SKILLS

Comprehension

- Analyze character
- Identify sequence of events

Word Study

- Adjectives that describe locations

Tier Two Vocabulary (see Glossary)

WRITING SKILLS

Writer's Tools

- Strong verbs

Writer's Craft

- How to write a biography

THEME CONNECTIONS

- **U.S. History**

*The reading level assigned to this text is based on the genre examples only. "Focus on the Genre," "Reread," and "Writer's Craft" features were not leveled. These sections are intended for read-aloud or shared reading.

Benchmark Education Company
145 Huguenot Street
New Rochelle, NY • 10801

Printed in Guangzhou, China.
4401/1219/CA21902059

ISBN: 978-1-60859-625-6

How to use this book

1. Learn about the genre by reading pages 2–3. Get background information about the subjects of the biographies on pages 4–5.
2. Read the biographies for enjoyment.
3. Reread the biographies and answer the questions on pages 13 and 21.
4. Reread the last biography. Pay attention to the comments in the margins. See how an author writes a biography.
5. Follow the steps on pages 22–23 to write your own biography.
6. Complete the activity on the inside back cover. Answer the follow-up questions.

Credits
Project Editor: Jeffrey B. Fuerst
Creative Director: Laurie Berger
Senior Art Director: Glenn Davis
Director of Photography: Doug Schneider
Photo Editor: Diane French
English Language Arts Advisor: Donna Schmeltekopf Clark

Photo credits: Cover B, Page 4B, 11, 12, 16, 17, 18, 20: The Granger Collection, New York; Page 8, 9: Library of Congress; Page 19: Bettmann/Corbis

Toll-Free 1-877-236-2465
www.benchmarkeducation.com
www.benchmarkuniverse.com

George Washington

Abraham Lincoln

Two Biographies

by Catherine Goodridge

Table of Contents

BIOGRAPHY

What is a biography?

A biography is a factual retelling of another person's life. The person may have lived long ago or in recent history, or the person may still be alive today. Biographies can cover a person's entire life, or just important parts of a person's life. When possible, a biography includes direct quotes from the person. This helps the reader make a connection to the person.

What is the purpose of a biography?

A biography helps a reader understand the people, places, times, and events that were or are important in the subject's life. It provides a summary of the person's major life experiences and achievements. In addition, the way the author writes the biography helps a reader get a sense of the person as a real human being who had (and perhaps still has) an impact on the lives of others.

How do you read a biography?

The title will tell you the subject of the biography and may include something interesting about him or her. The first paragraph will try to "hook" the reader by capturing his or her attention. As you read, note the setting. The setting often influences what happens in a person's life. Also pay close attention to the sequence of events in the person's life. Ask yourself: *Did this event happen to the person, or did the person make it happen? How did this event affect the person's life? What do I admire about this person? Is there something in this person's experiences that I could apply to my life?*

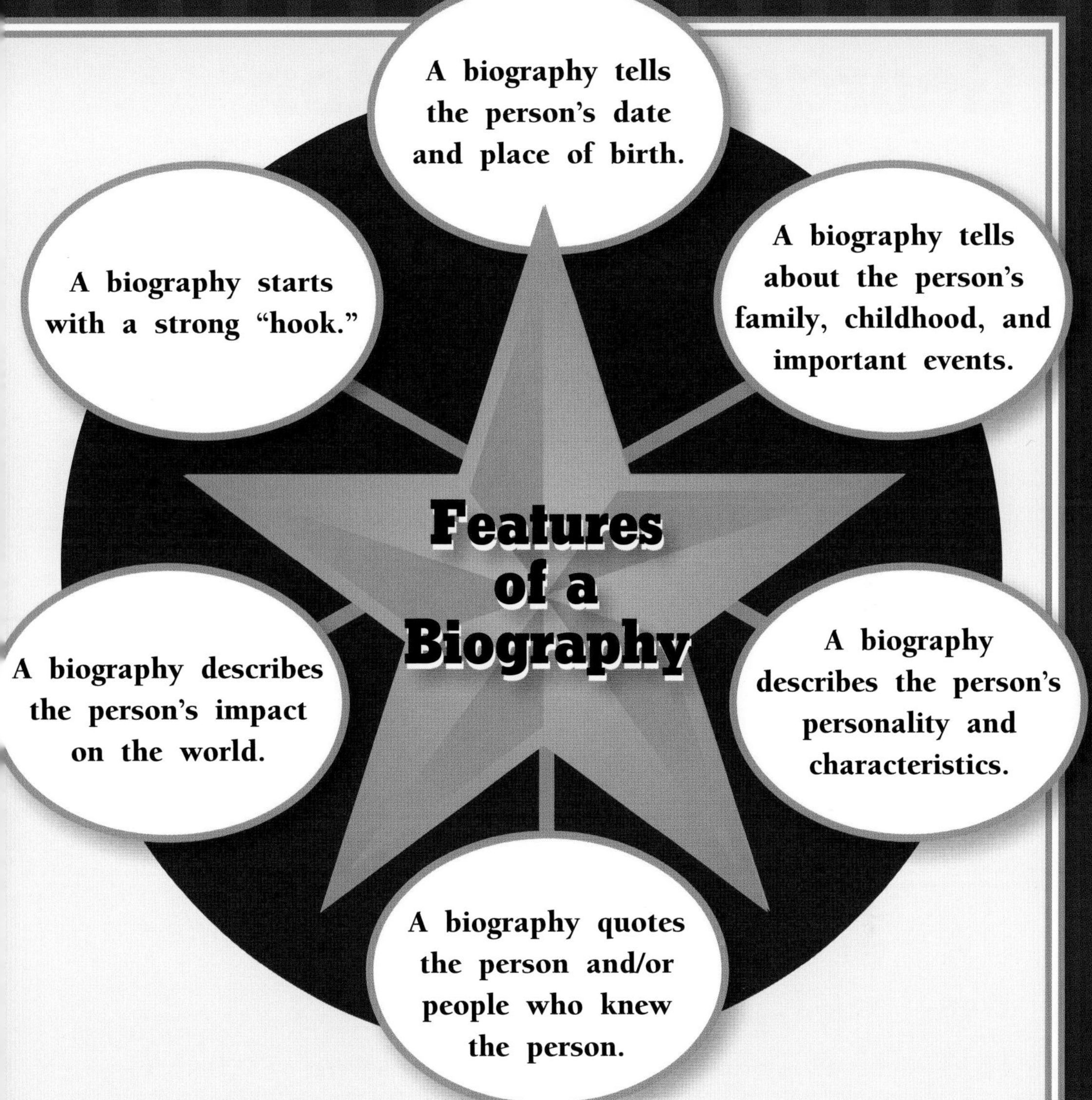

Features of a Biography

A biography tells the person's date and place of birth.

A biography tells about the person's family, childhood, and important events.

A biography describes the person's personality and characteristics.

A biography quotes the person and/or people who knew the person.

A biography describes the person's impact on the world.

A biography starts with a strong "hook."

Who writes biographies?

People who write biographies want to learn more about others' life stories and how those people made their marks on the world. Some people write biographies because they are interested in a certain topic, such as sports, history, or cooking. Others write biographies simply because they are interested in people!

Meet the Subjects

George Washington and Abraham Lincoln

George Washington	
1732	Born on February 22 in Virginia.
1748	Became a surveyor.
1753	Served as a soldier in the French and Indian War.
1759	Married Martha Dandridge Custis, a widow with two children.
1775	Chosen to lead the colonists' war with Britain.
1777	Endured a difficult winter in Valley Forge, Pennsylvania, with his loyal soldiers.
1781	Helped the colonies win their freedom from Britain.
1789	Became the first President of the United States.
1799	Died at his home in Mount Vernon, Virginia.

Abraham Lincoln	
1809	Born on February 12 in Kentucky.
1837	Started a law practice in Illinois.
1842	Married Mary Todd.
1843, 1846	Had two sons.
1847	Won election to U.S. Congress.
1850, 1853	Had two more sons.
1861	Became sixteenth President of the United States; the Civil War began.
1863	Signed the Emancipation Proclamation to free slaves.
1865	Civil War ended; Lincoln was assassinated.

Tools Writers Use

Strong Verbs

Which sounds better: "I talked loudly" or "I shouted"? Yes, **shouted** is a stronger verb, or action word. **Shouted** doesn't need an adverb, such as **loudly**, to make it better. We already know that shouting is loud. Another way to use strong verbs is to choose synonyms that specifically describe an action. These words help show, rather than tell, what happened. For example, do you walk to class, or do you stride, amble, shuffle, or saunter? Finally, authors use strong verbs to shorten, or tighten, sentences. Example: "I designed the poster" (verb: **designed**) rather than "I was the designer of the poster" (verb: **was**).

George Washington

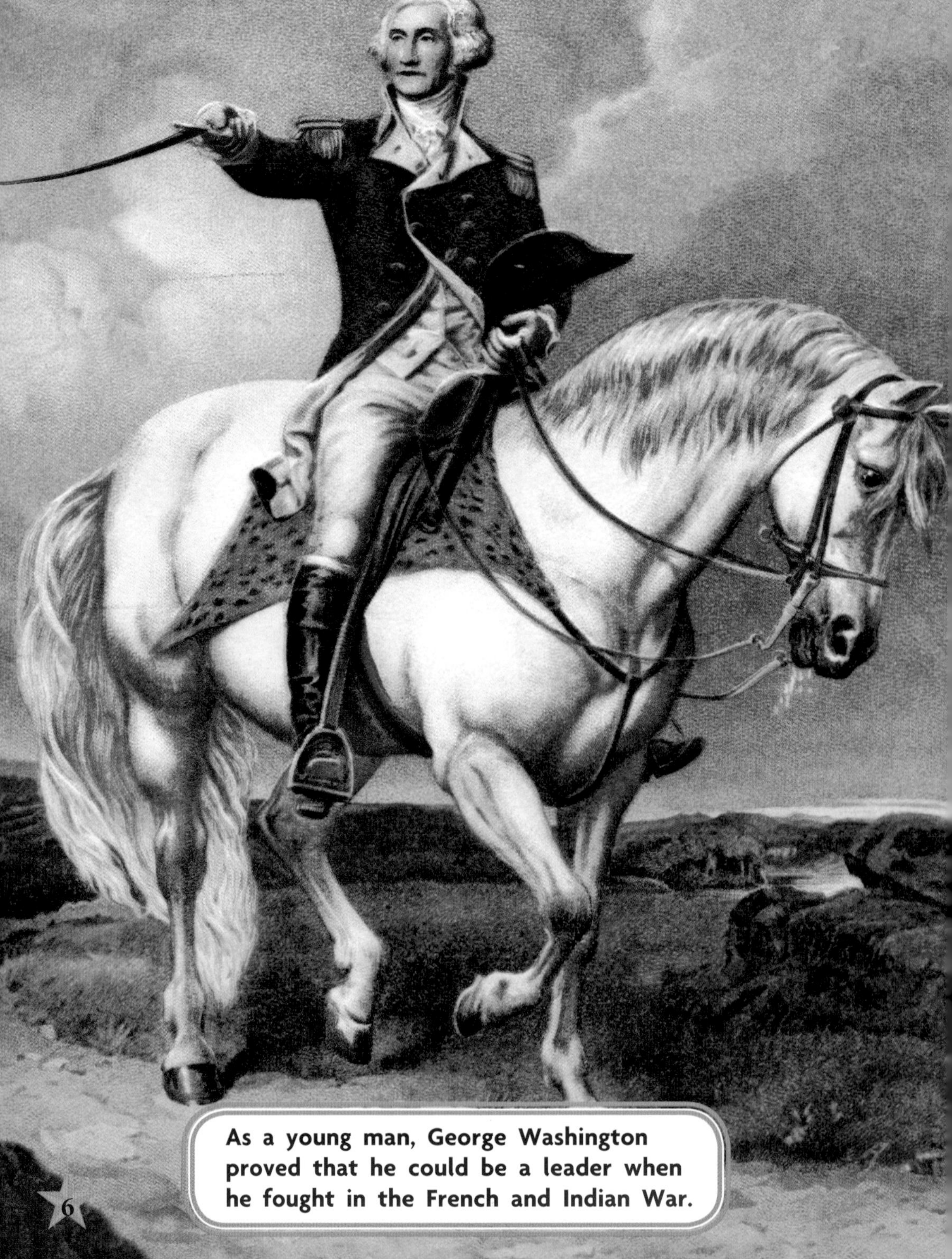

As a young man, George Washington proved that he could be a leader when he fought in the French and Indian War.

Only one person in the history of the United States is known as the "Father of Our Country." That person is George Washington. Few people have ever served their country as well as George Washington. He was a soldier, a general, and a leader. He was the first president of a new country.

Life in Virginia

George Washington was born on a large farm in Virginia on February 22, 1732. As a boy, George loved the **open** fields and **mysterious** forests. He liked to hunt and to ride horses. He liked to farm the **fertile** land of his home.

When he was a young man, George became a surveyor. He measured land and made maps. He went deep into the wilderness of Virginia. He camped and learned to take care of himself in dangerous situations.

When George was just twenty-one years old, he became a soldier. He fought with the British against the French. George proved himself to be a strong leader. He earned a promotion to colonel.

In 1759, George married. He and his wife Martha settled down to a quiet life. They lived on a **spacious** farm called Mount Vernon. He filled his days by running the farm, hunting, fishing, and helping to raise Martha's two children. But these happy and peaceful times did not last.

Revolution!

By 1775, there were thirteen colonies. The people who lived in the colonies followed laws made by the British king, George III. They paid taxes to Britain. The colonists wanted to choose their own leaders and make their own laws. They wanted to make their own decisions about taxes. They wanted their own government.

Leaders from the colonies met in Philadelphia to talk about what to do. These leaders made an important decision: They would separate from Britain. They would fight for freedom if they had to.

In April 1775, the colonies went to war with Britain. To fight, they had to form an army. They chose George Washington to lead it. He was forty-three years old.

George Washington took part in the decision to declare independence.

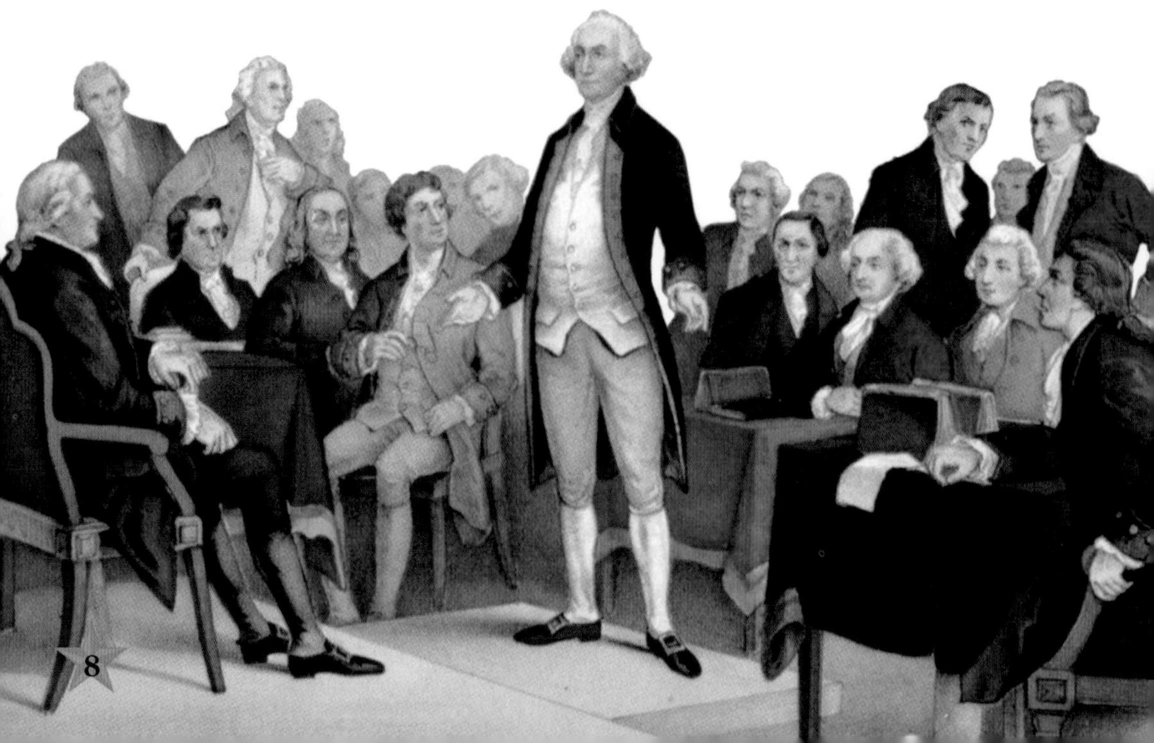

Leader in War

Washington's army faced great hardship at Valley Forge, Pennsylvania, during one cold winter of the Revolution.

Washington had been a hero in the French and Indian War twenty years earlier. Now he would fight against the British as General George Washington. Few generals ever faced a greater challenge. The British had the strongest army and the biggest navy in the world. How could thirteen small colonies defeat them?

The revolution was long and bloody. Most of Washington's soldiers had little training. Washington sometimes had no money to pay them. Supplies were short. It was often hard to get food. How did a small, poorly trained army fight the awesome military power of Britain? They had Washington as their leader!

To build a better army, Washington used the skills he developed in the wilderness of Virginia. He taught his men to travel light and to move quickly and quietly. He showed them how to hide in the woods. He made surprise attacks on the enemy.

Washington's men loved him and would do anything for him. He did not let them give up and he did not give up himself. He begged for supplies for his men. He once wrote that the men had "not even the shadow of a blanket" to keep warm in the bitter cold. The British had a large army, but the United States had George Washington.

At first, Washington's army suffered many defeats. Holding his men together was difficult. During the terrible winter of 1777, Washington and his soldiers camped in the icy snow at Valley Forge, Pennsylvania. Many soldiers had no shoes or warm clothing. They were hungry. Even Washington grew discouraged.

"I am wearied almost to death," he wrote. Many of his soldiers were ready to give up and leave for home. But Washington and his soldiers stayed to fight on.

In 1781, after six years of fighting, the colonies won their freedom. The United States of America was born.

A New Leader for a New Country

Washington said that the only reward he wanted for his hard work was the "affection of a free people." He returned to a quiet life at Mount Vernon. He expected to spend the rest of his days there. But again his peaceful farming life did not last. His country was forging a new nation. The country needed a leader with courage and strength. The people wanted someone with common sense and experience. Washington was the ideal choice.

The United States was a new country with a new set of laws. The people had a new way of governing. Instead of having a king, they would vote for a leader. Washington was the one man everyone trusted to get the new government started. "Liberty, when it begins to take root, is a plant of rapid growth," he wrote to James Madison in March 1788. Washington won the election and became president of the new nation.

On April 30, 1789, George Washington stood on the balcony of Federal Hall in New York City. It was a cloudless day. Thousands of people lined the narrow streets. They cheered and tossed flower petals. Cannons boomed. Washington placed his hand on a Bible and repeated an oath of office. He promised to "preserve, protect, and defend the Constitution of the United States." He was the first person to make this promise.

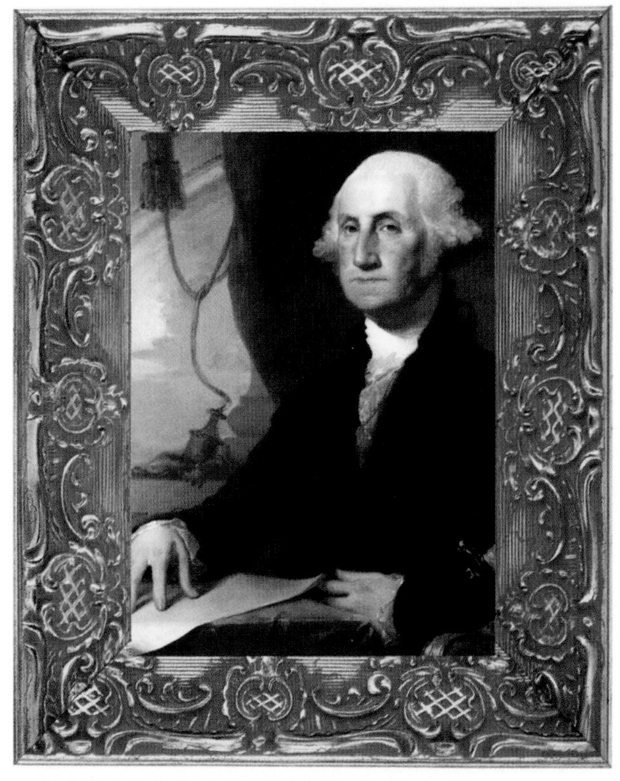

This is a famous painting of the first President of the United States.

Washington was president for a term of four years. Then he served for a second term. He proved that a president chosen by the people could be a good leader. He worked to make the new nation strong. During his time in office, five new states joined the Union. He made new laws for the new country. He signed treaties, or agreements, with other countries. He helped the states work together as one government. He kept the nation out of war.

Home Again

When he left office, Washington returned to his **beloved** home. After the excitement of war and the presidency, he was glad to enjoy the peaceful life of Mount Vernon again. He often told people that he liked to be thought of as the "nation's first farmer." He died at Mount Vernon on December 14, 1799.

George Washington was born to a simple, quiet life. He led his country through a long and dangerous war. He guided it through the early years of freedom. When he died, the following words were spoken about him in a speech delivered before Congress by General Henry Lee: "He was first in war, first in peace, and first in the hearts of his countrymen."

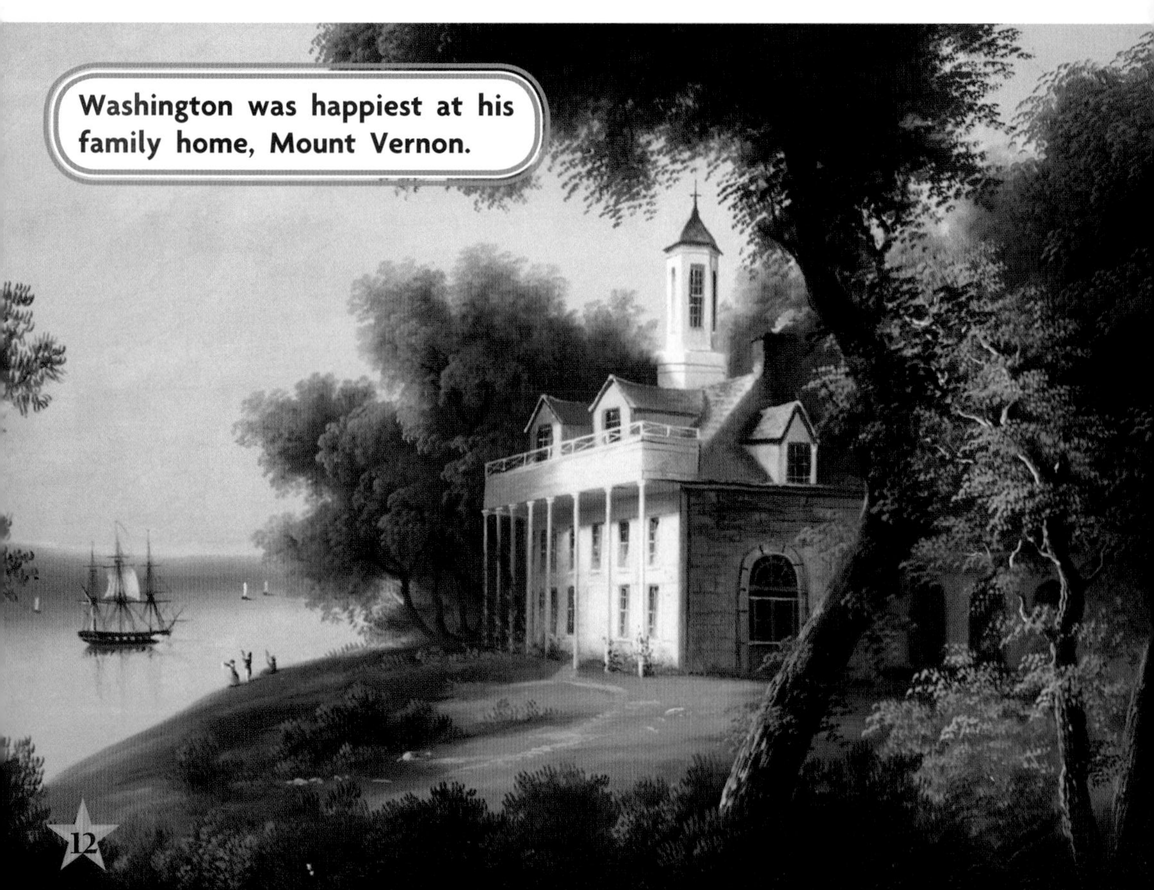

Washington was happiest at his family home, Mount Vernon.

Reread the Biography

Analyze the Subject

- George Washington was resourceful, meaning he knew how to use his skills to get what he needed. How can you tell? Identify two examples.
- What were some of Washington's accomplishments?
- What things were important to George Washington?

Analyze the Tools Writers Use

Strong Verbs

Reread the sentences with the following verbs. What do these verbs tell you about George Washington?

- measured, camped, fought, earned
  ("Life in Virginia," page 7)
- developed, taught, showed, suffered, stayed
  ("Leader in War," pages 9–10)
- expected, promised, served, worked, signed
  ("A New Leader for a New Country," pages 10–11)

Focus on Words

Adjectives That Describe Locations

Adjectives give more information about nouns and pronouns. They answer questions such as *what kind of, which,* and *how many*. Authors use adjectives to describe settings, or locations. Make a chart like the one below. What can you figure out about the following locations in the biography of George Washington?

Page	Phrase	Adjective	Noun Described	Question the Adjective Answers
7	open fields			
7	mysterious forests			
7	fertile land			
7	spacious farm			
12	beloved home			

The title tells whom the biography is about.

The author "hooks" the readers in the first paragraph. Readers will want to learn more about the great person who has such a big statue. What did he do that so many people visit his statue every year?

Abraham Lincoln

Every year, thousands of people climb the marble steps of the Lincoln Memorial in Washington, D.C. They look up at a large and **grand** statue of President Abraham Lincoln, the sixteenth President of the United States. The words written on the walls say that his memory will live forever in the hearts of the people.

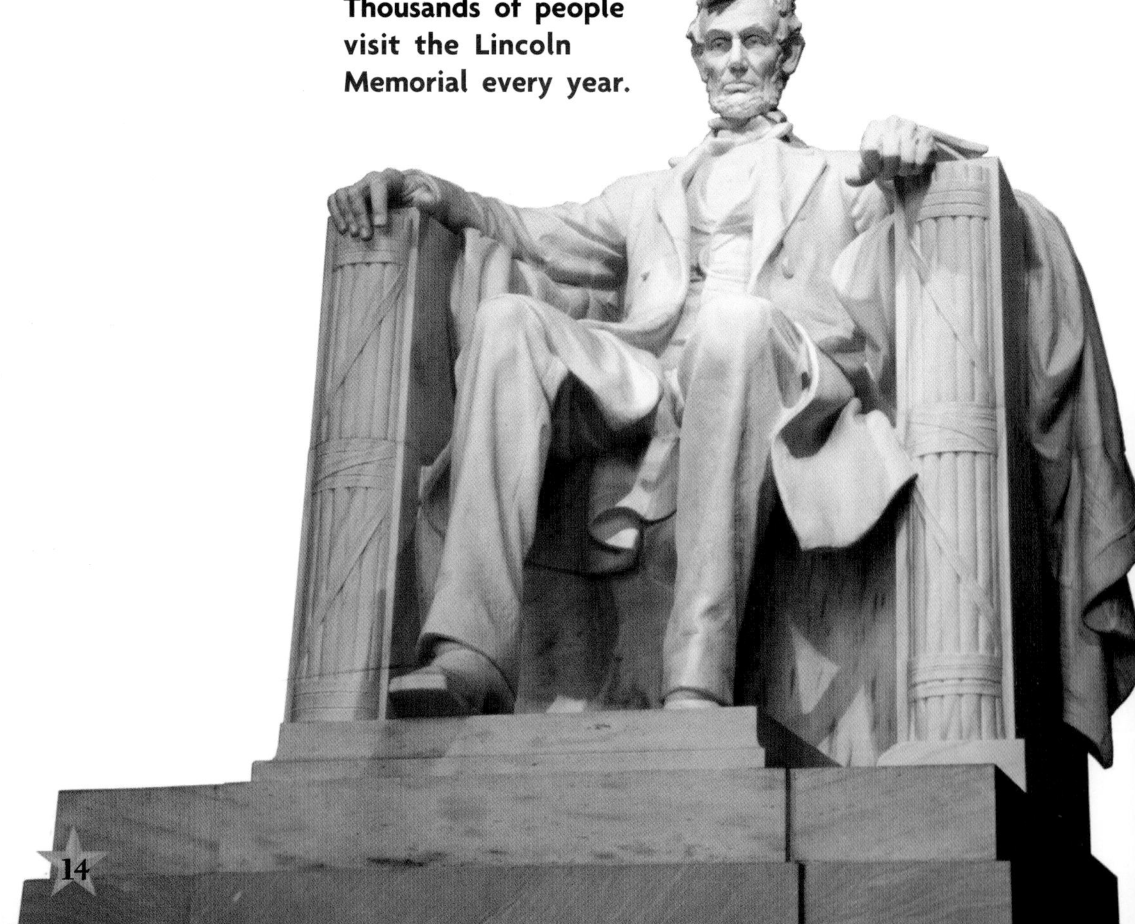

Thousands of people visit the Lincoln Memorial every year.

Early Days

Abraham Lincoln was born in Kentucky on February 12, 1809. He lived with his family in a rough and **rugged** cabin that Abe's father built. His parents had no schooling, but they shared what they knew. In the evenings by the fire, Abe's mother told Bible stories. His father told tall tales.

Soon the Lincolns moved to Indiana, which was a wilderness. They cleared away some of the **dense** forest on a plot of land and started a farm. Young Abe learned to plant, harvest, catch fish, and split rails for fences.

A biography needs to include the date and place of birth of the subject. Note that the author uses adjectives to describe the places Lincoln lived. These descriptions help readers picture the places in their own minds.

Reading and Writing

Abe went to school only when he was not needed on the farm—and when a teacher was available. Still, he did very well in school. He treasured every moment that he could spend reading. "The things I want to know are in books," he said.

When Abe was nine, his mother died. His father remarried. Sally Lincoln had no schooling, but she had books that she shared with Abe. In the evenings, he often read aloud to his family.

The author tells about the people and key events in Lincoln's early life. The reader sees that Lincoln faced difficulties. Knowing that he struggled when growing up, which happens to all people, makes readers get a good feeling about him.

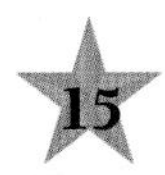

Abraham Lincoln

Abe and his stepmother grew very close. Sally believed that he would do great things someday.

Abe could read, but most of his neighbors could not. Many of them stopped by the cabin to ask for his help. He read their letters, their bills, and their important papers. He wrote letters for them. He saw that under their smiles, people had troubles. Some had worries, others had debts; some were homesick, others were ill.

Illinois

In 1831, the Lincolns moved to Illinois. Abe, now an adult, helped his father clear land and build a new cabin. Then he set out on his own. Farming was not what he wanted.

Abe had grown to be a tall, serious man. He was slow to make up his mind, but he made good decisions. His talent for telling funny stories made him many friends. He worked on the river, in a store, and in a post office. Folks who knew him said that he once overcharged someone by six cents and then walked miles to give it back. This story may not be true—but he did have the nickname "Honest Abe."

The author shows different sides of Lincoln's personality. He was hardworking. He had a good sense of humor. He cared about people.

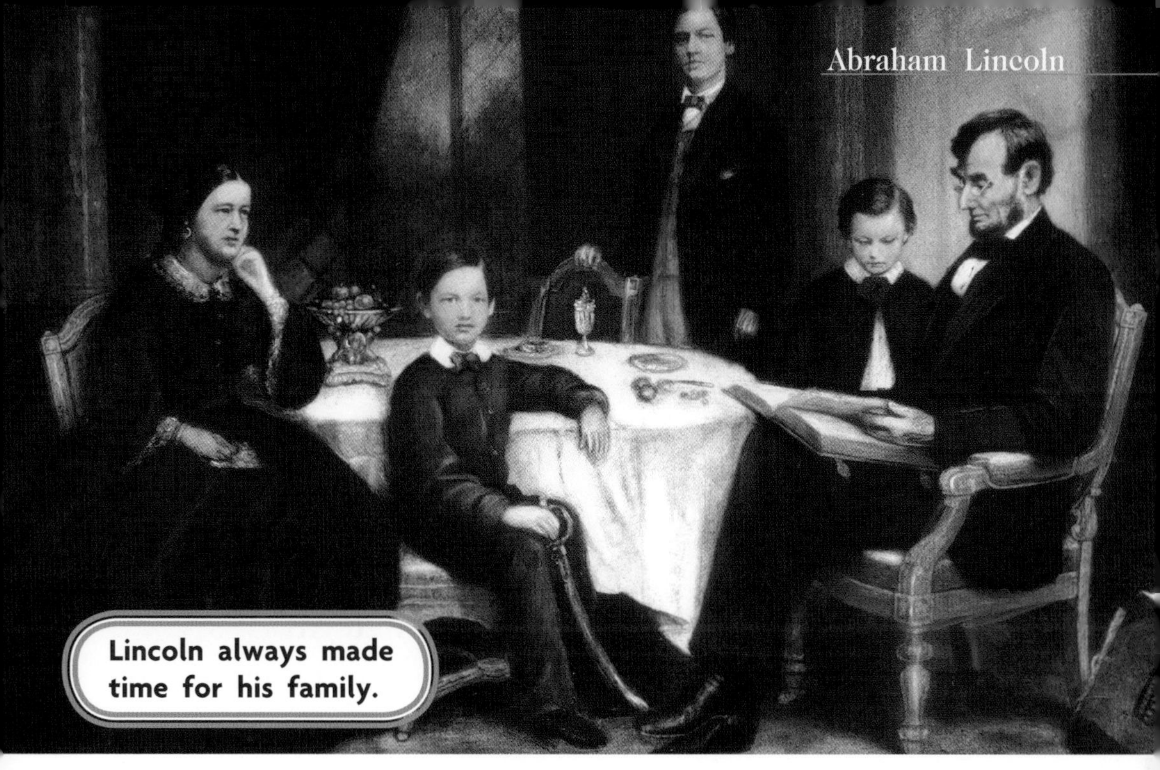

Lincoln always made time for his family.

In 1842, Abe married Mary Todd. They moved to Springfield, Illinois, a small but **expanding** city, and started a family. Lincoln had trained himself in law by reading on his own. In Springfield, he set up a law practice.

He prospered and soon began to think about how to serve his country. He was elected to the U.S. House of Representatives in 1847. When he ran for the Senate in 1854, he lost the election. But Lincoln was an electrifying speaker and a brilliant writer. The speeches he made showed people that he shared their troubles and understood their needs. He showed that he had the skills and talent to be a great leader.

The author uses strong verbs to tell the story. Prospered means "to get rich."

The author tells about some of Lincoln's accomplishments. Now readers get a better idea of why he is a good person for a biography.

Civil War

In 1860, Lincoln ran for president. This decision came at a dangerous time in the United States. A war between the states was coming. At the time, many Southerners owned slaves. Most Northerners were against slavery. People in Southern states grew angry over attempts to keep slavery from spreading to the territories, or new states. They began to think about forming their own government. They wanted to make a new nation where slavery would be legal.

Lincoln won the election of 1860. He believed that all states must be willing to obey the laws of the country, and that no state had the right to break up the Union.

More than 600,000 Americans died in the Civil War.

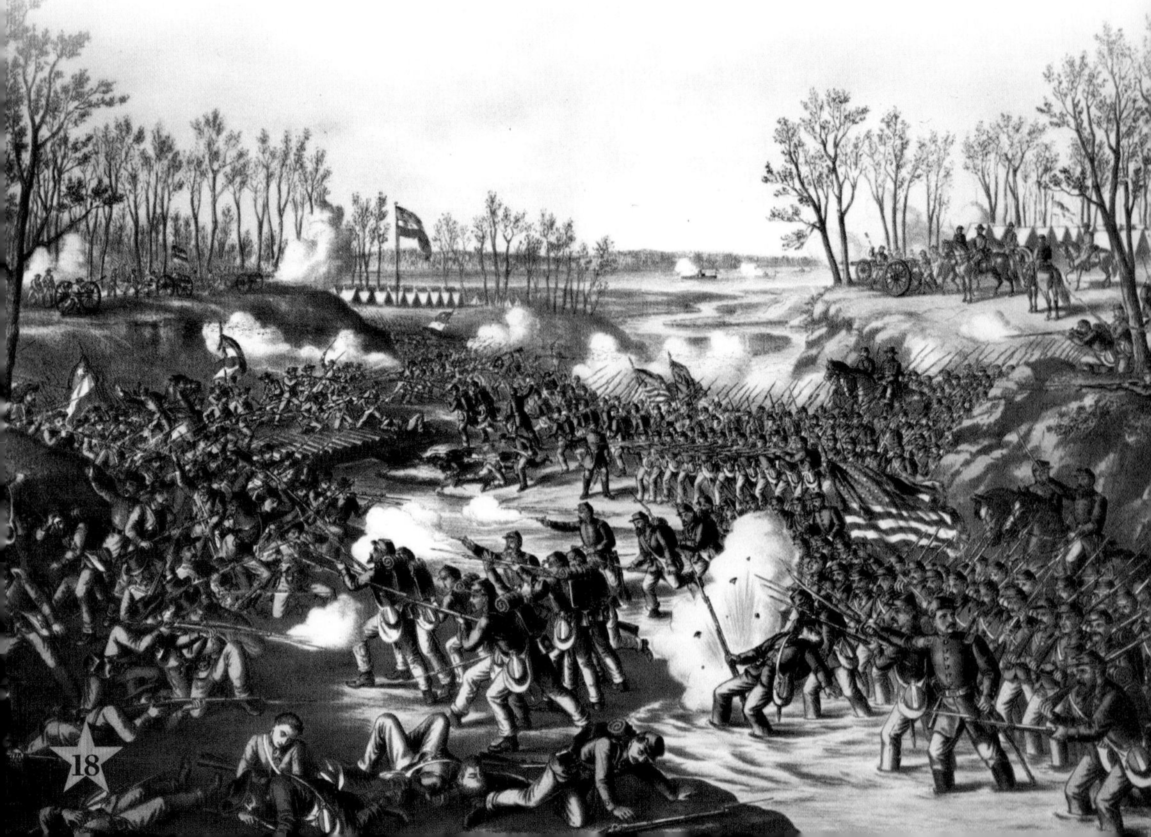

In a famous speech, Lincoln said, "A house divided against itself cannot stand." If it took a war to save the country, then he would go to war.

Soon after the election, the Southern states decided to secede, or to separate themselves from the Union. On April 12, 1861, the Civil War began.

Lincoln met often with Generals Sherman and Grant during the Civil War.

Forever Free

On January 1, 1863, while the war was still raging, Lincoln took steps to end slavery. He signed an important document. It was the Emancipation Proclamation. It declared that enslaved people living in Southern states would be "thenceforth, and forever free." Lincoln knew that the signing was an important event. He said, "If ever my name goes into history, it will be for this act, and my whole soul is in it."

The author includes a quote from Lincoln. Quotes help readers connect to the subject of the biography. They also show the subject's personality.

In 1864 the end of the war was close. Lincoln again ran for president and won. He spoke about the peace that the country needed. He urged all Americans to work together to heal the wounds of war "with malice toward none; with charity for all."

Abraham Lincoln

Victory came on April 9, 1865. Eleven Southern states had fought against the twelve Northern states. After four years, the North had won. Lincoln had saved the Union and ended slavery. He now made plans to reunite the nation.

Abraham Lincoln did not live to see his dreams come true. On the evening of April 14, 1865, a gunshot rang out at a theater in Washington, D.C.

Lincoln died several hours after he was shot. He was killed by an unhappy Southerner named John Wilkes Booth. A special train took Lincoln's body back to Illinois. People stood by train tracks all along the journey to honor him.

Nearly 150 years later, Abraham Lincoln is still one of his country's most beloved leaders. He took office as the nation was breaking apart. As president, he brought that nation back together. Without Lincoln, there might not be a United States of America today.

The author concludes with some more reasons why Lincoln is important and a good subject for a biography.

Reread the Biography

Analyze the Subject

- Abraham Lincoln was principled, meaning there were things he believed in strongly. How can you tell? Identify two examples.
- What are some of Lincoln's accomplishments?
- Who or what most influenced Lincoln in his life? How?

Analyze the Tools Writers Use

Strong Verbs

The author uses strong verbs to describe Lincoln's actions. Reread the sentences with the following verbs. What do these verbs tell you about him?

- cleared, plant, harvest, catch, split ("Early Days," page 15)
- treasured, read, wrote ("Reading and Writing," pages 15–16)
- helped, worked, trained, prospered, showed ("Illinois," pages 16–17)
- signed, declared, urged, saved, reunite ("Forever Free," pages 19–20)

Focus on Words

Adjectives That Describe Locations

Adjectives can answer *what kind of*, *which*, and *how many* questions about locations. Make a chart like the one below. What can you figure out about the following locations in the biography of Abraham Lincoln?

Page	Phrase	Adjective	Noun Described	Question the Adjective Answers
14	grand statue			
	rugged cabin			
15	dense forest			
15	expanding city			

How does an author write a BIOGRAPHY?

Reread "Abraham Lincoln" and think about what Catherine Goodridge did to write this biography. How did she describe Abraham Lincoln's life? How did she show what he accomplished?

Decide on Someone to Write About

Remember: A biography is a factual retelling of someone's life. Therefore, you must either interview the person or research his or her life. In "Abraham Lincoln," the author wanted to tell about Mr. Lincoln's path from being a young boy in Kentucky to having a memorial built in his honor in Washington, D.C.

Decide Who Else Needs to Be in the Biography

Other people will likely be an important part of your subject's life. Ask yourself:

- Who was in the person's family?
- Who were the person's friends and neighbors?
- Who did the person go to school with or work with?
- Who helped or hurt the person?
- Which people should I include?
- How will I describe these people?

Person or Group	How They Impacted Abraham Lincoln's Life
family	cared for him; told him stories; read with him; taught him to work hard
neighbors	depended on him to help them read important papers and write letters
Southerners	many did not agree with his beliefs about slavery

Recall Events and Setting

Jot down notes about what happened in the subject's life and where these things happened. Ask yourself:

- Where did the person's experiences take place? How will I describe these places?
- What were the most important events in his or her life?
- What situations or problems did the person experience?
- What did the person accomplish?
- What questions might my readers have about the subject that I could answer in my biography?

Subject	Setting	Important Events
Abraham Lincoln	Kentucky; Indiana; Illinois; Washington, D.C.	1. He lived in a rugged cabin in Kentucky as a boy.
		2. He trained himself to become a lawyer.
		3. He was elected President of the United States.
		4. He helped save the Union and end slavery.

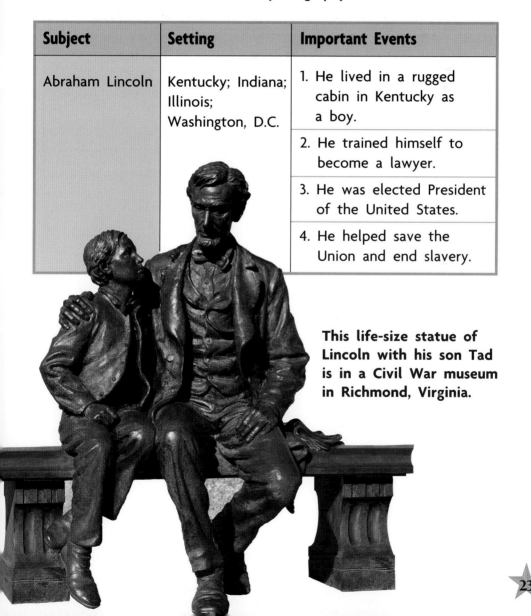

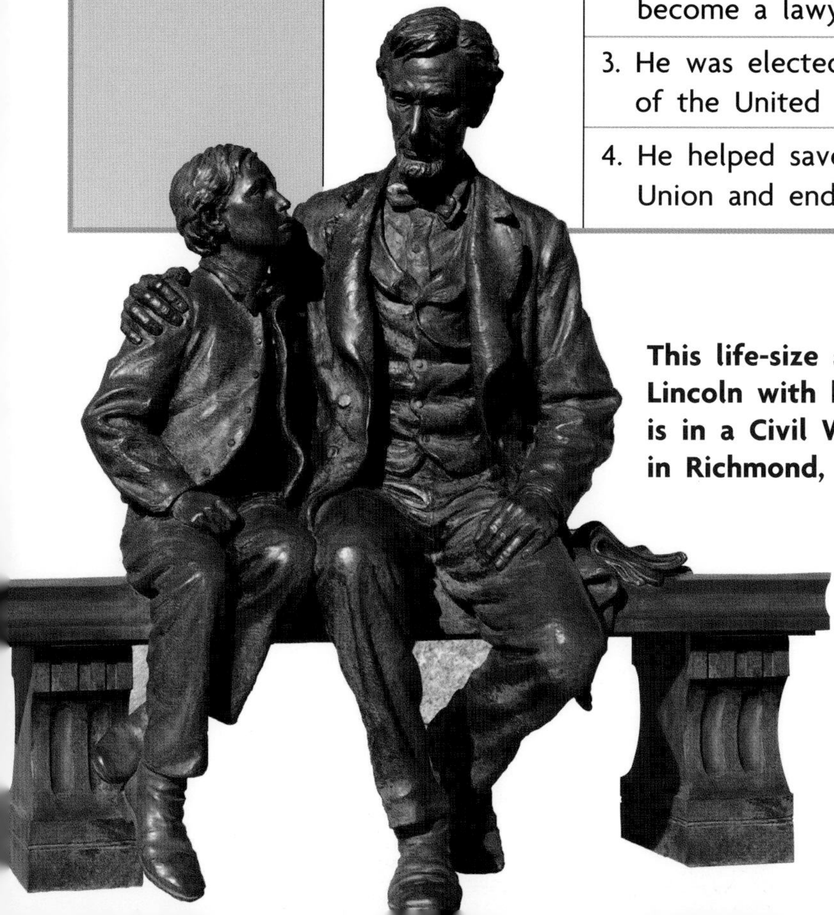

This life-size statue of Lincoln with his son Tad is in a Civil War museum in Richmond, Virginia.

Glossary

beloved (bih-LUVD) dearly loved; dear to the heart (page 12)

dense (DENS) crowded together (page 15)

expanding (ik-SPAN-ding) growing bigger (page 17)

fertile (FER-tul) good for plants or crops to grow in (page 7)

grand (GRAND) big in size and dignified in appearance (page 14)

mysterious (mis-TEER-ee-us) spooky and interesting (page 7)

open (OH-pen) without barriers or fences (page 7)

rugged (RUH-ged) rough and strong (page 15)

spacious (SPAY-shus) vast; big; roomy (page 7)

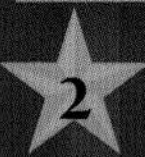

How does an author write a BIOGRAPHY?

Reread "Abraham Lincoln" and think about what Catherine Goodridge did to write this biography. How did she describe Abraham Lincoln's life? How did she show what he accomplished?

1. Decide on Someone to Write About

Remember: A biography is a factual retelling of someone's life. Therefore, you must either interview the person or research his or her life. In "Abraham Lincoln," the author wanted to tell about Mr. Lincoln's path from being a young boy in Kentucky to having a memorial built in his honor in Washington, D.C.

2. Decide Who Else Needs to Be in the Biography

Other people will likely be an important part of your subject's life. Ask yourself:

- Who was in the person's family?
- Who were the person's friends and neighbors?
- Who did the person go to school with or work with?
- Who helped or hurt the person?
- Which people should I include?
- How will I describe these people?

Person or Group	How They Impacted Abraham Lincoln's Life
family	cared for him; told him stories; read with him; taught him to work hard
neighbors	depended on him to help them read important papers and write letters
Southerners	many did not agree with his beliefs about slavery

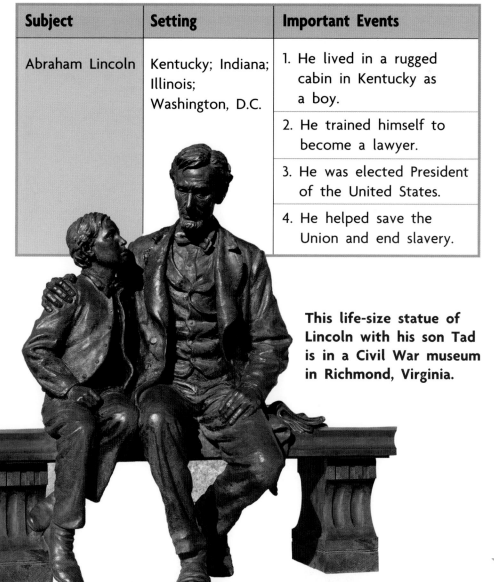